ZOMBIES

COMING SOON ZOMBIE APOCALYPSE

James A. York

ISBN: 9781693837395

First Print Edition: 09,2019

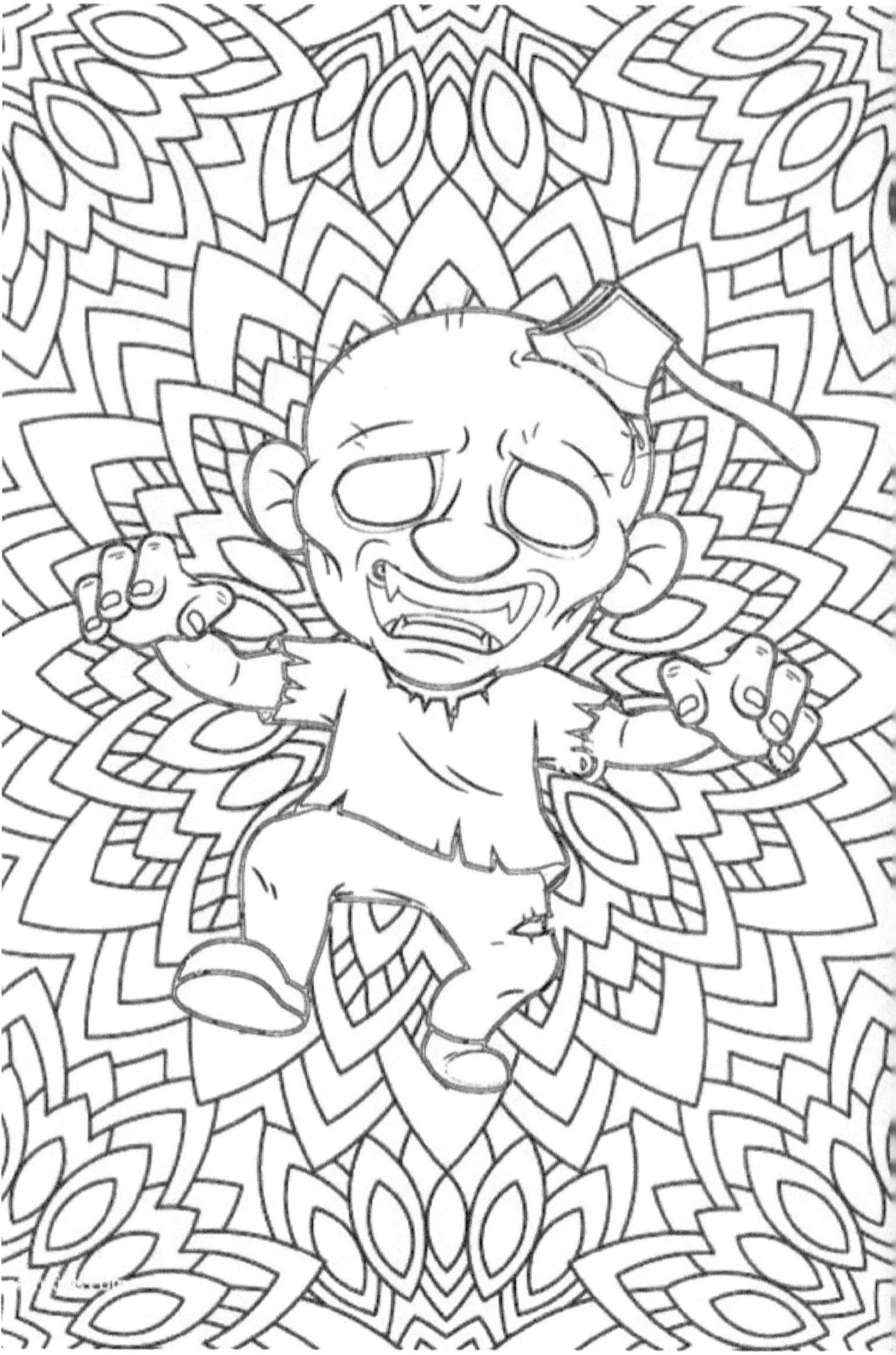

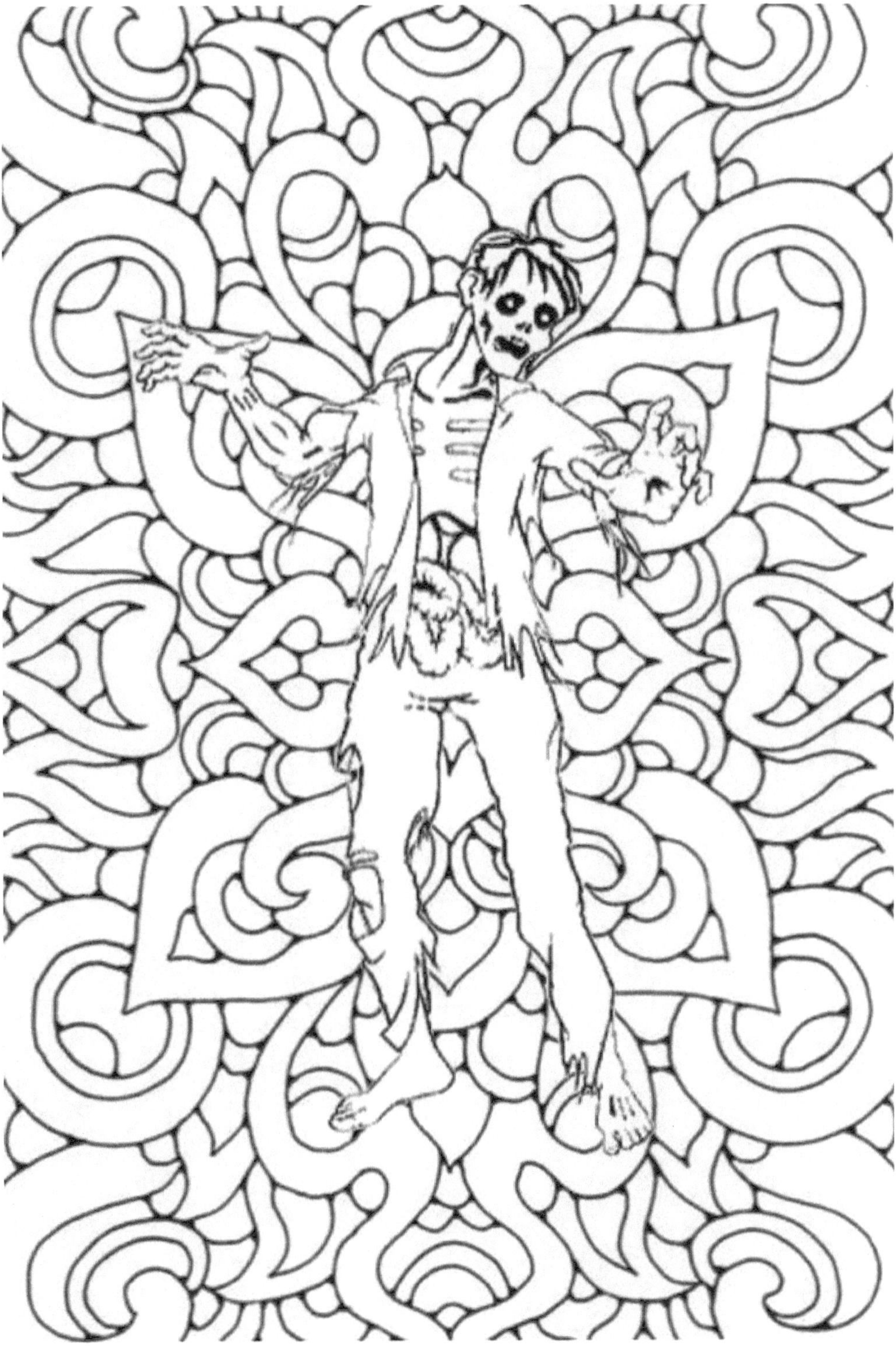

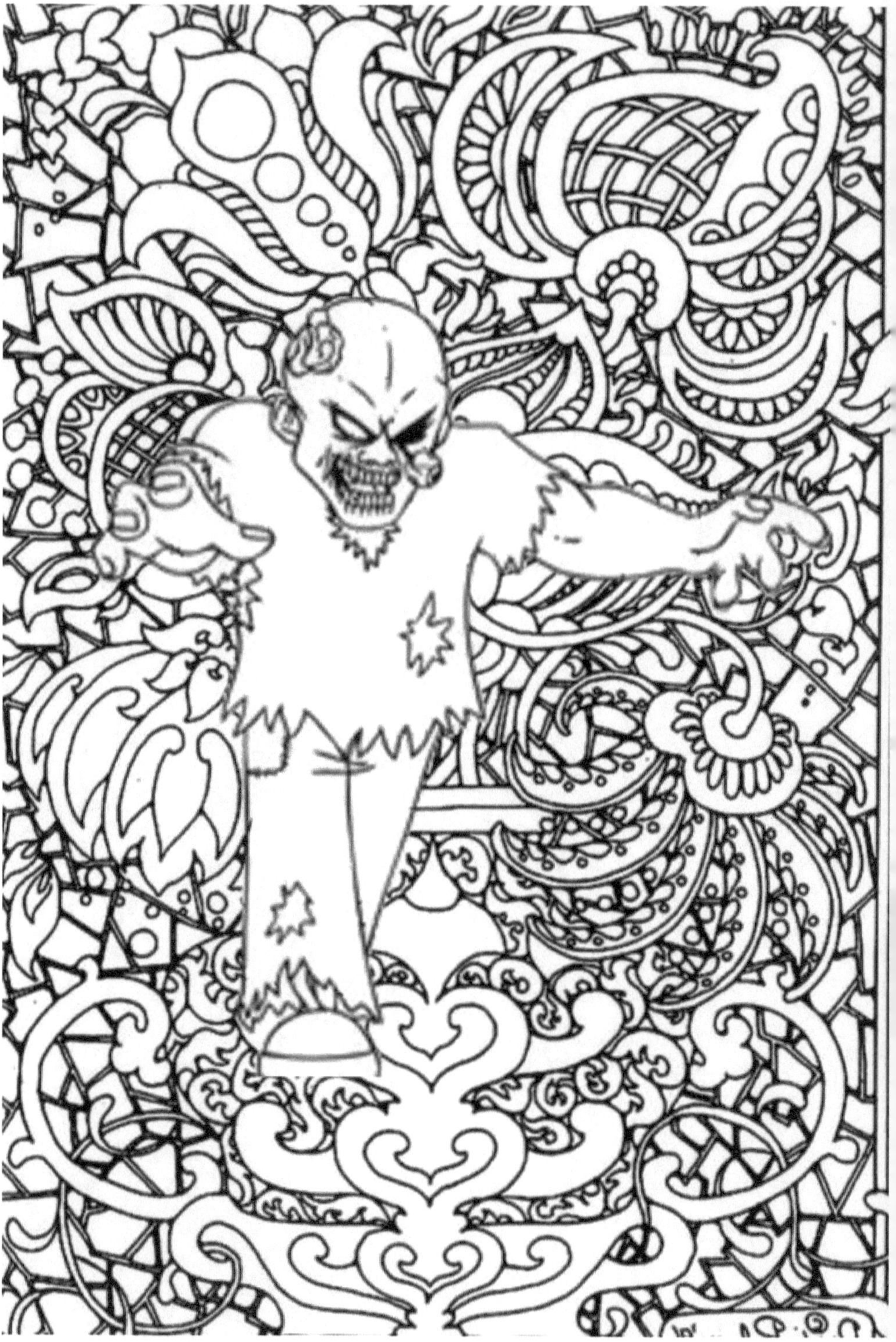

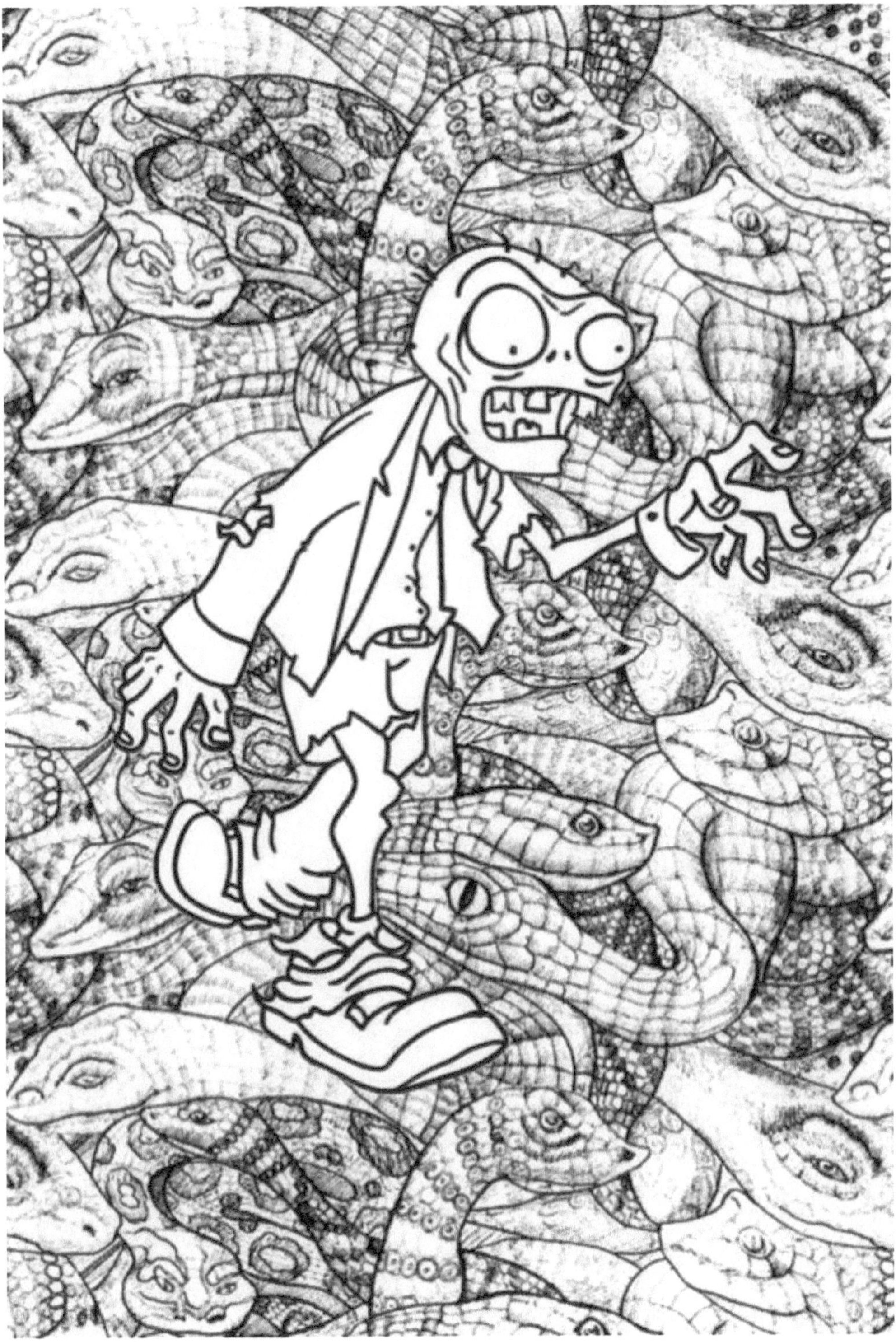

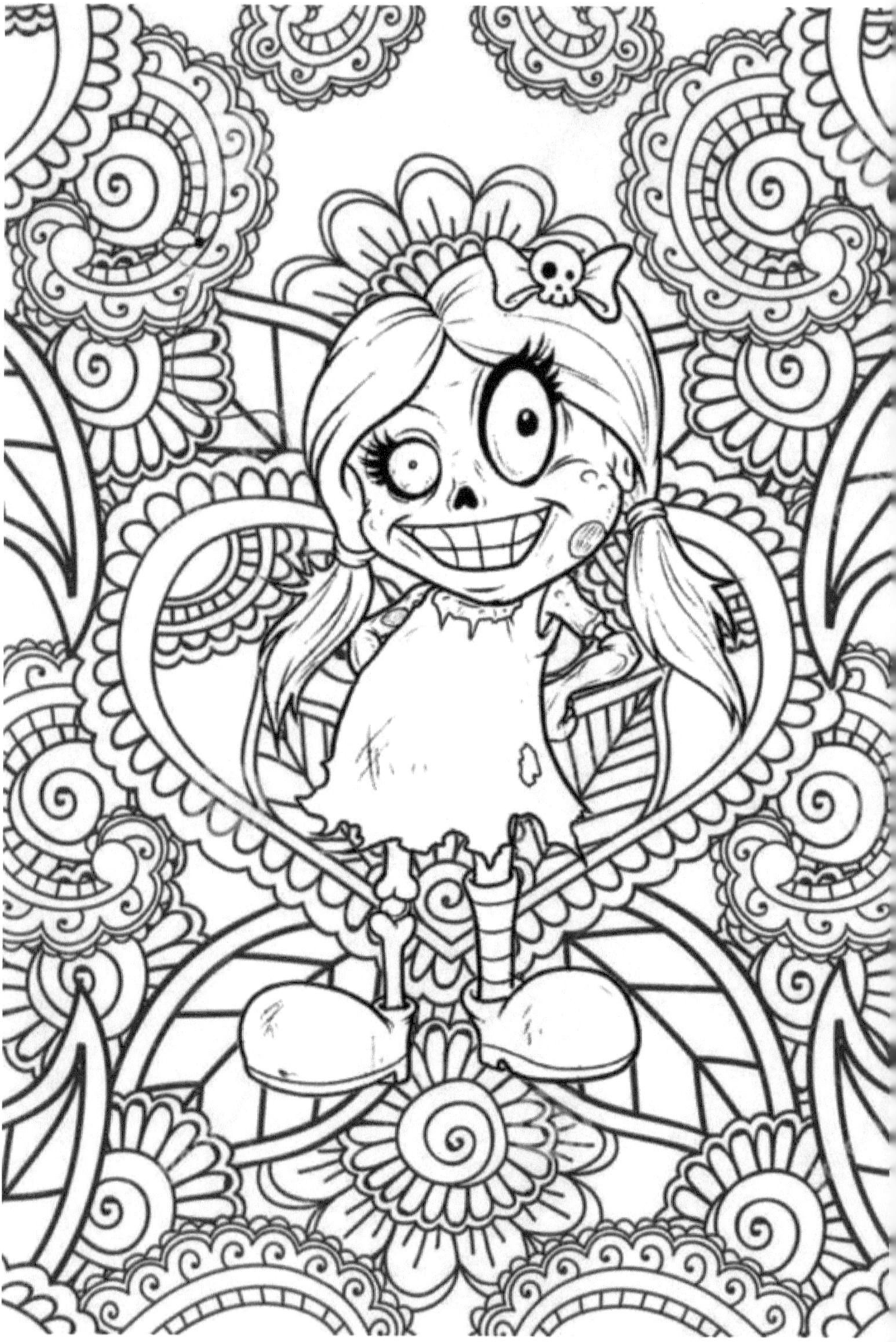

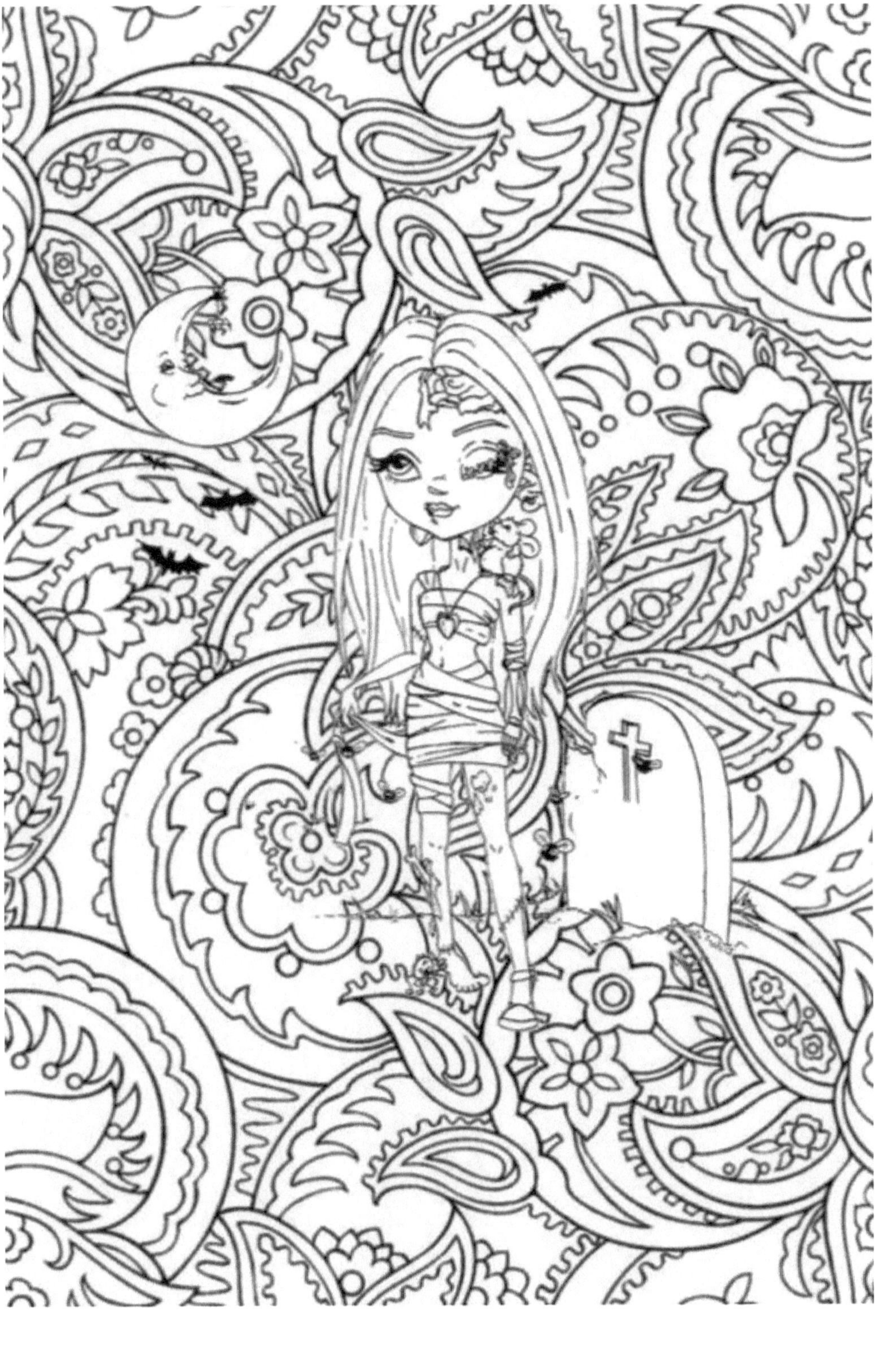

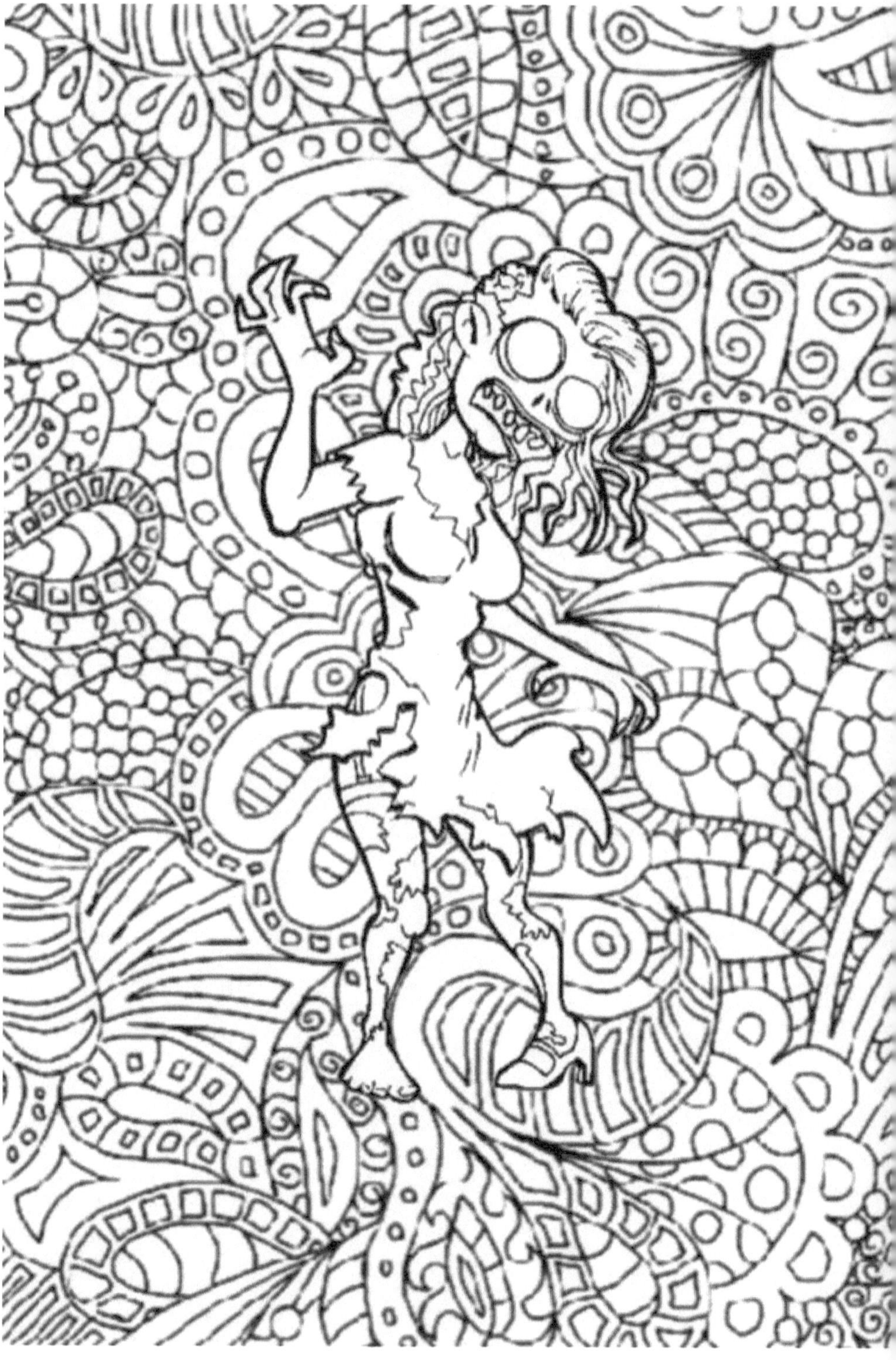

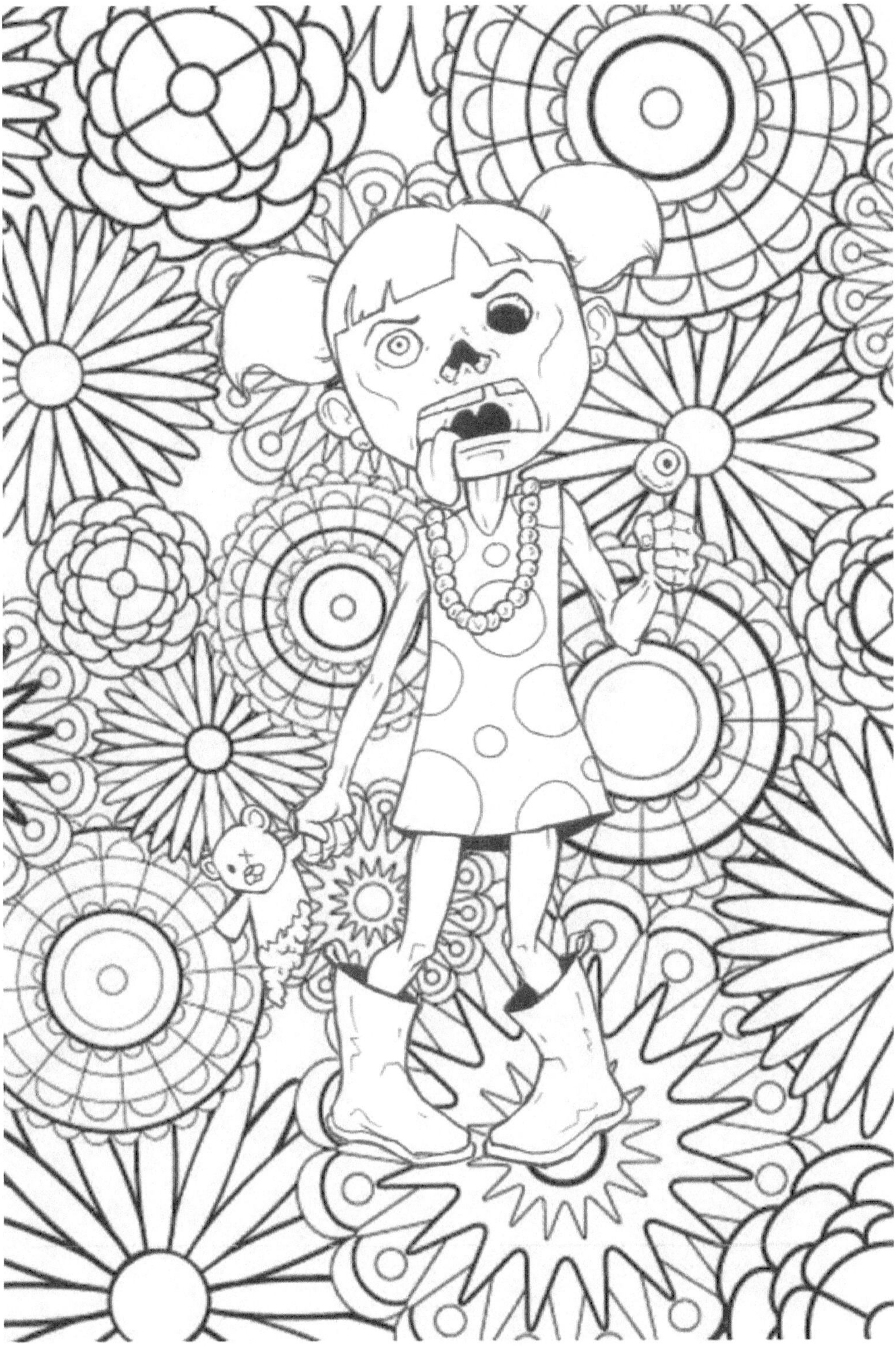

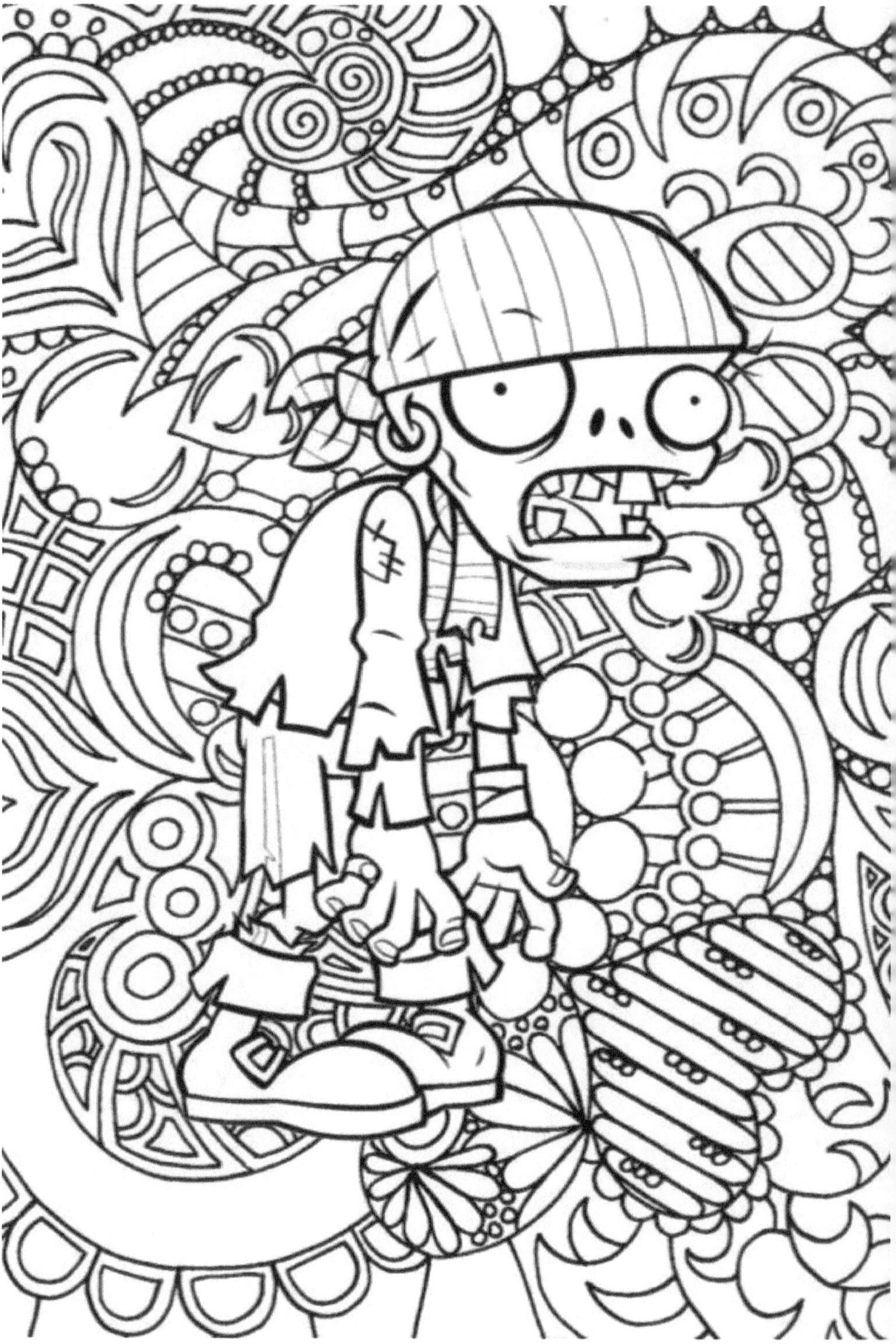

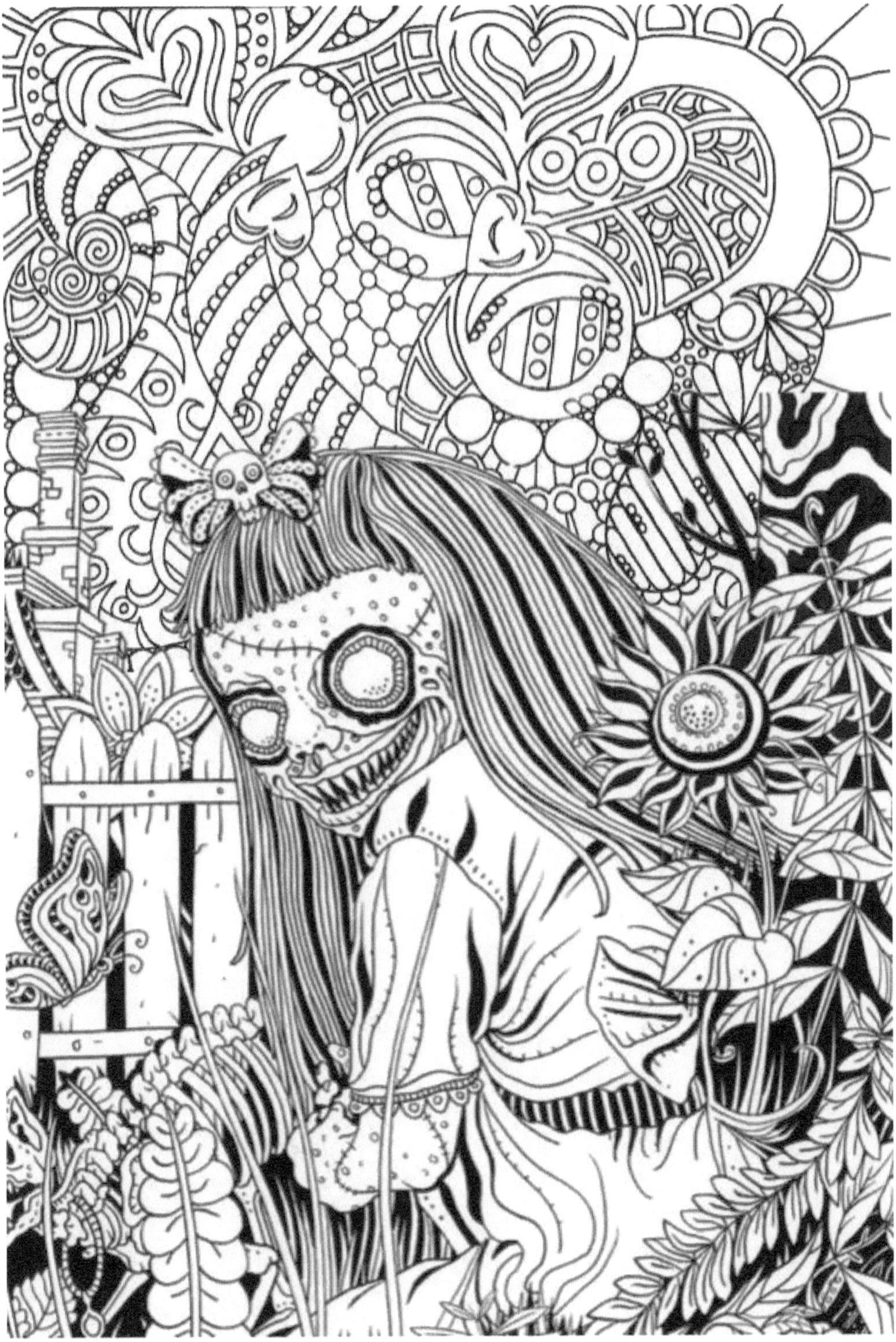

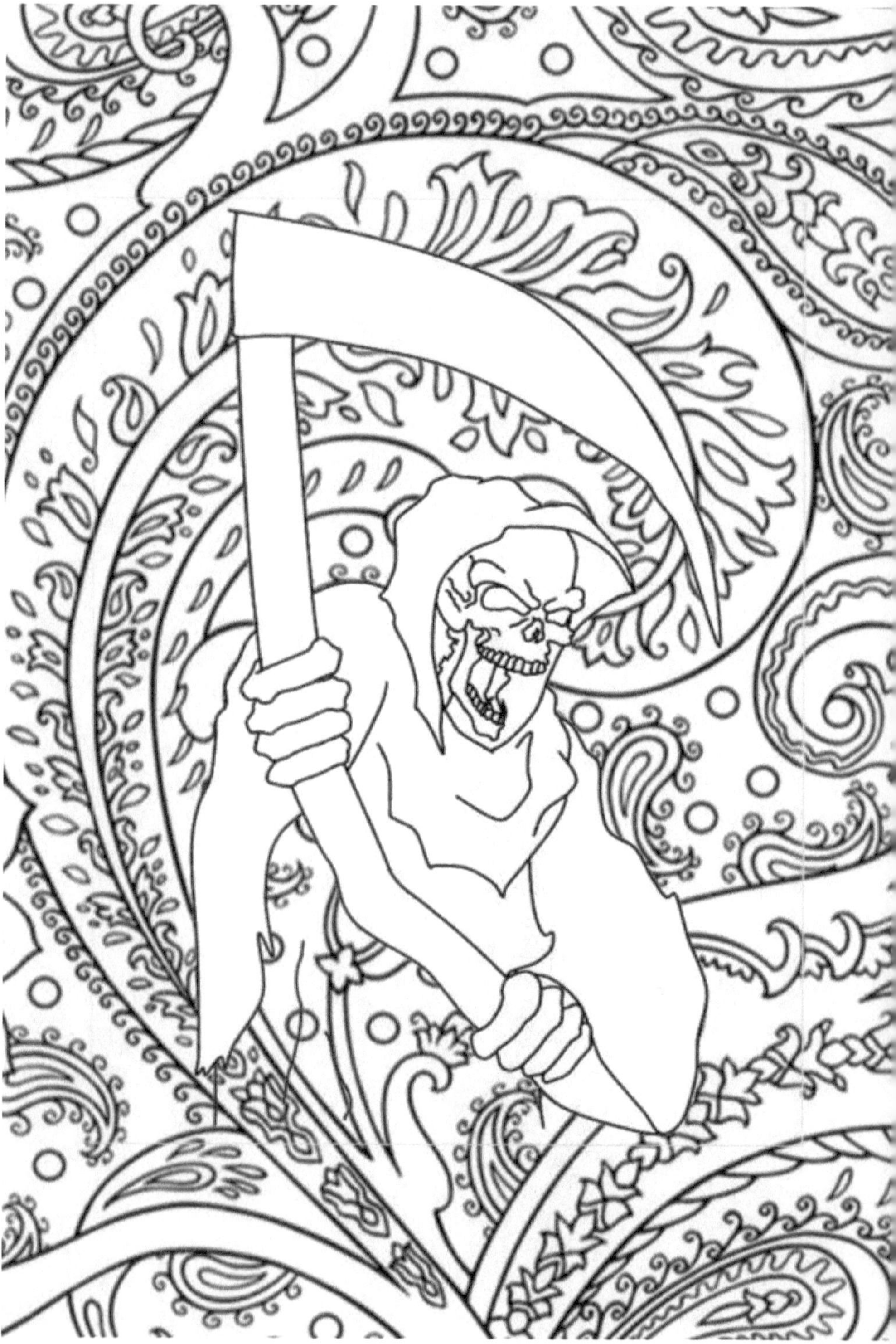

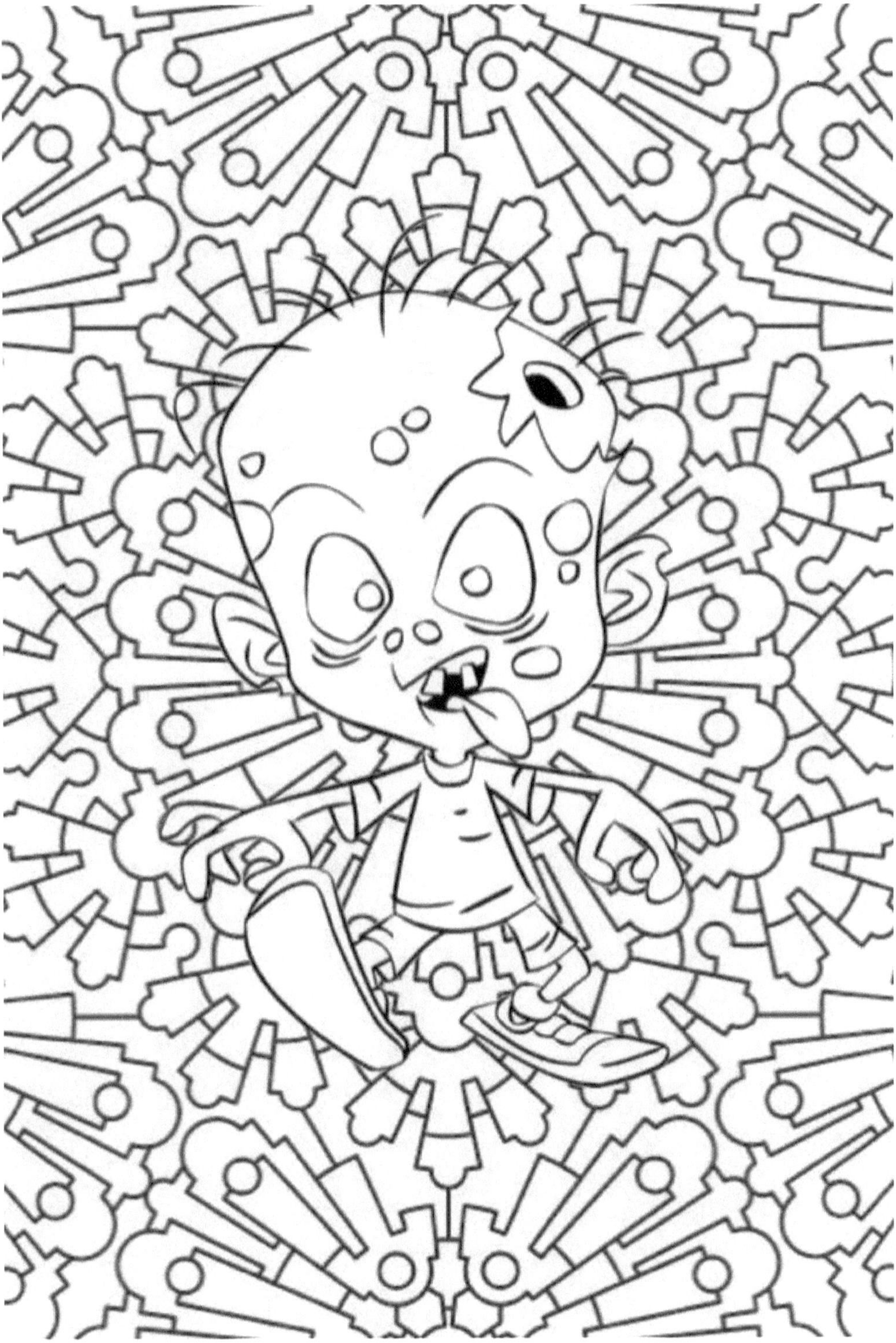

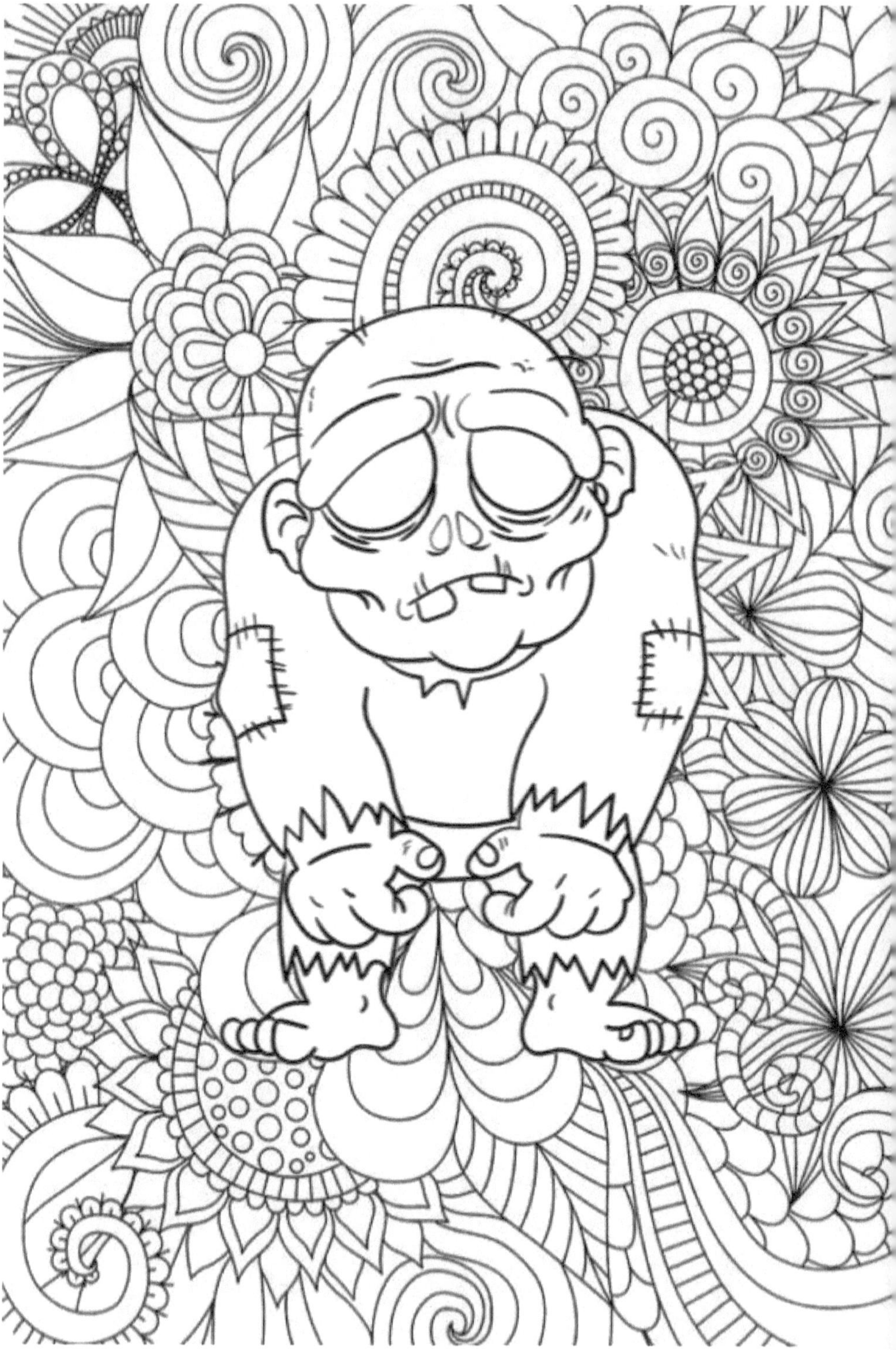

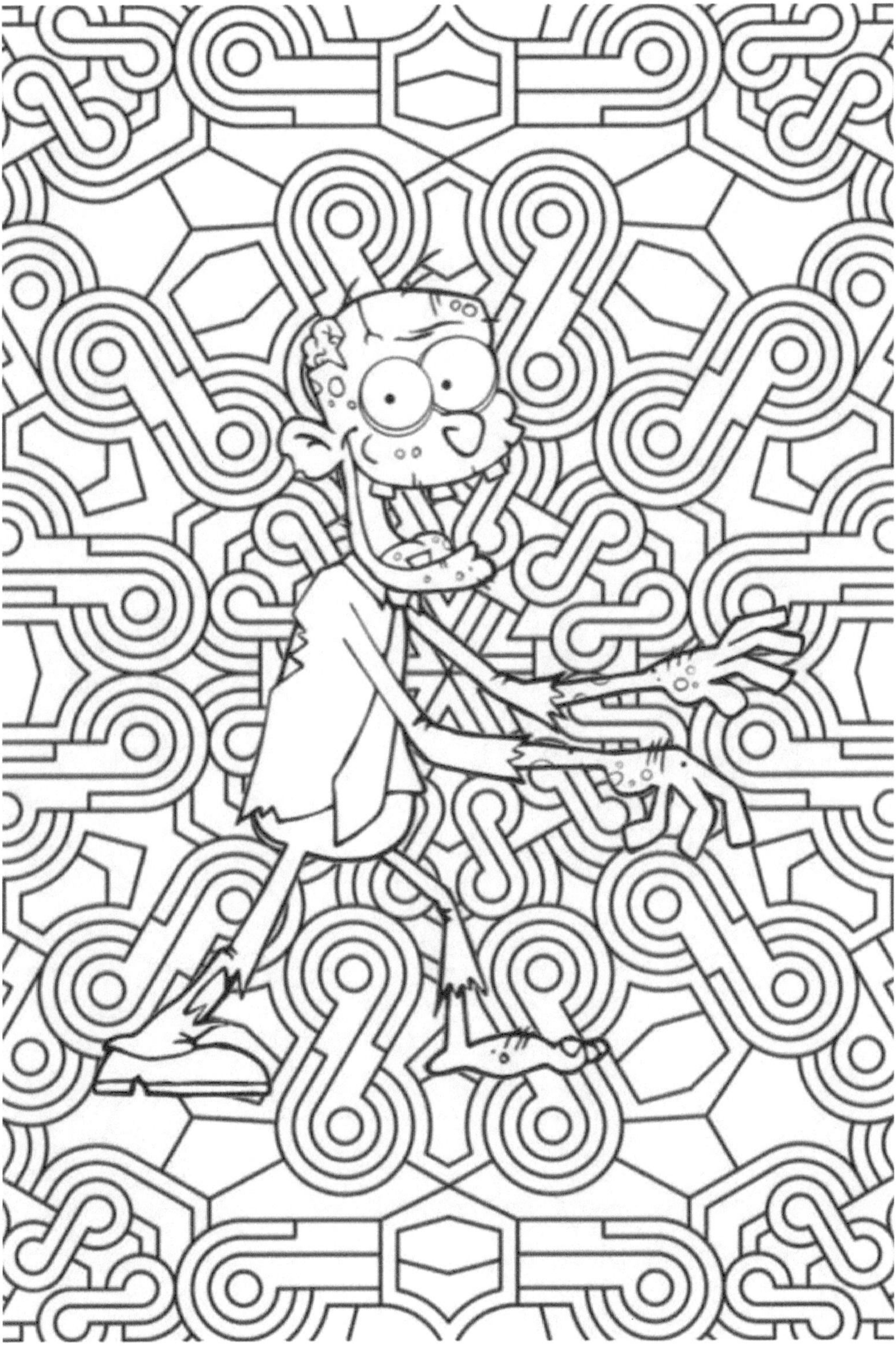

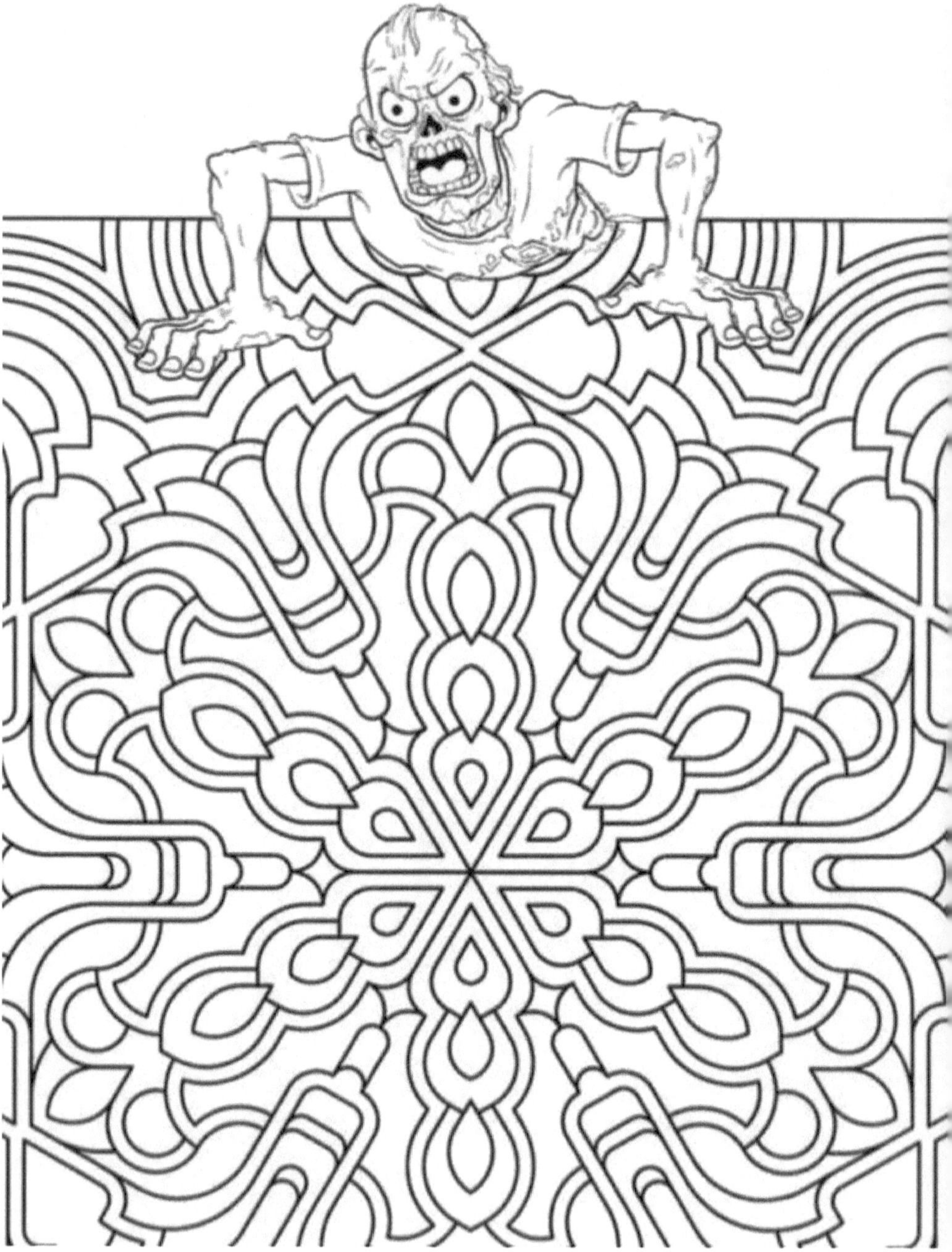

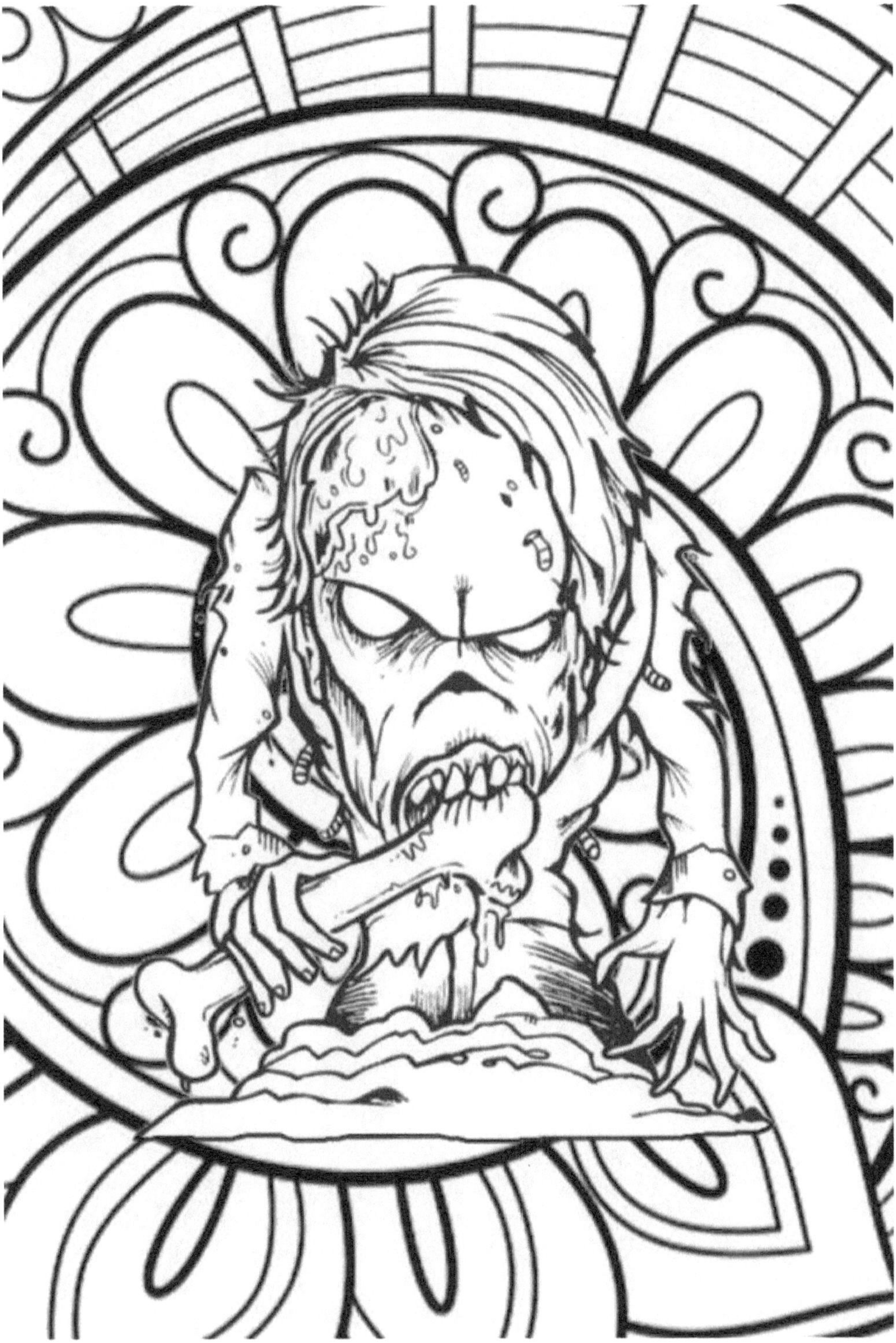

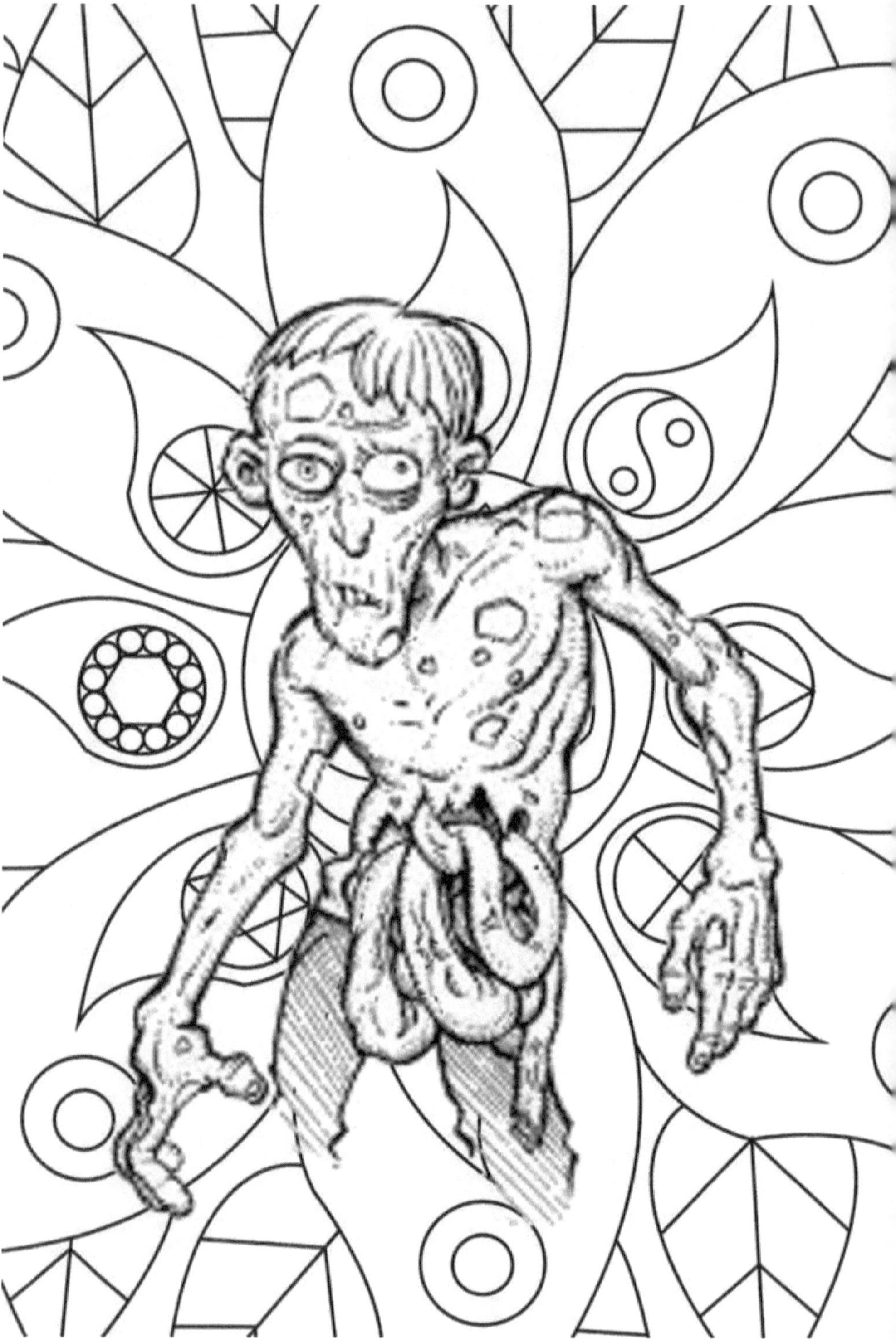

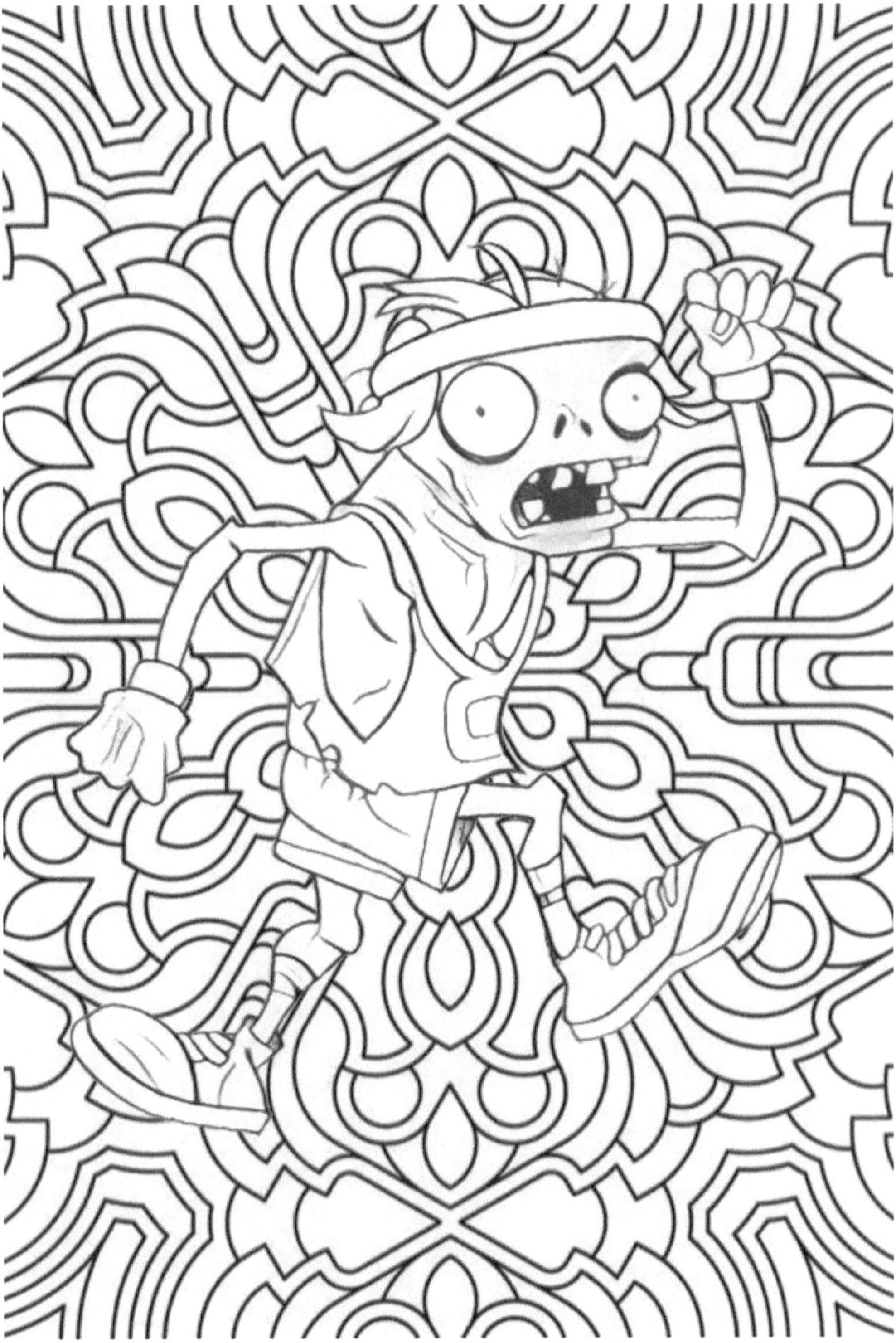

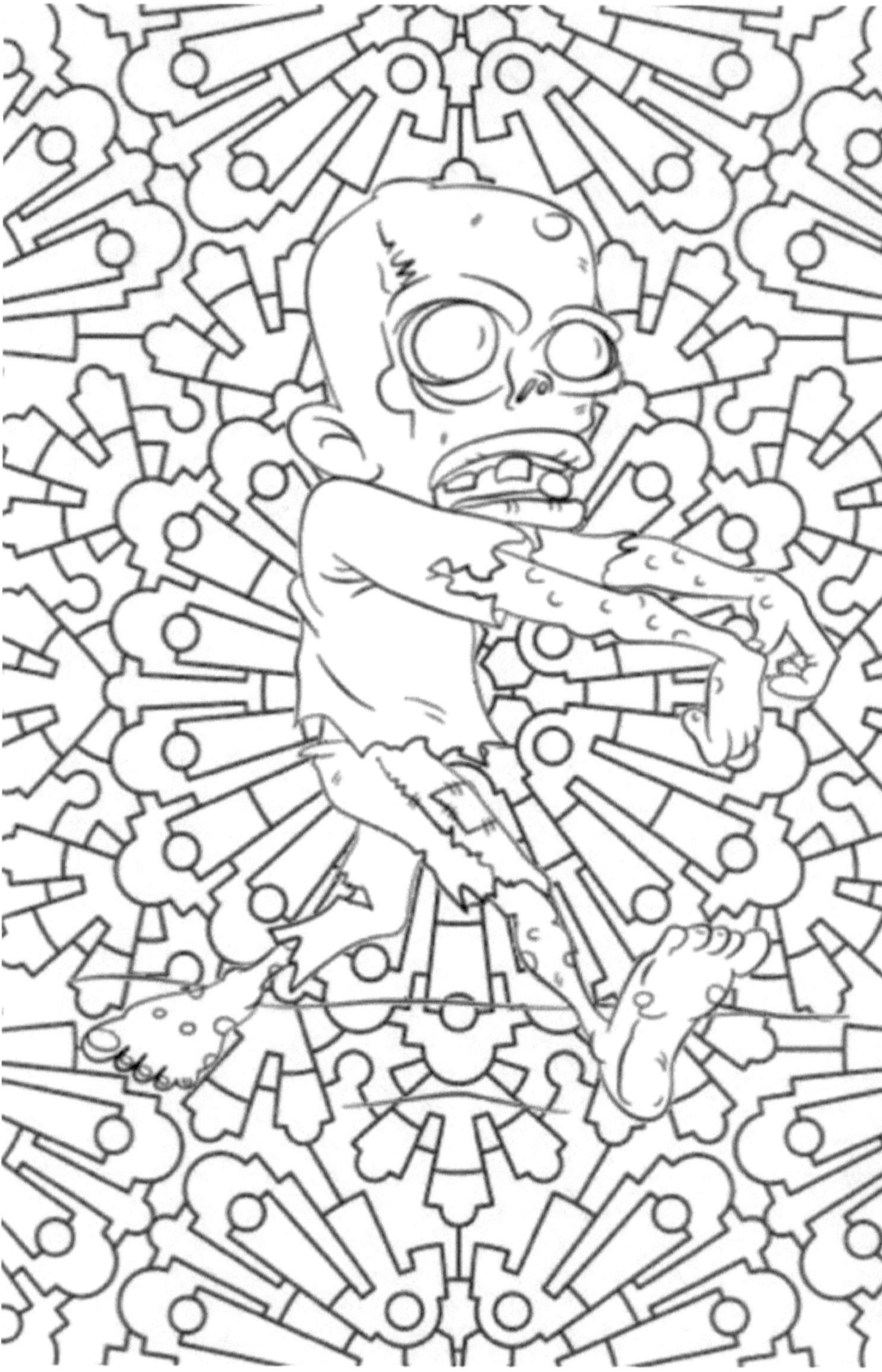

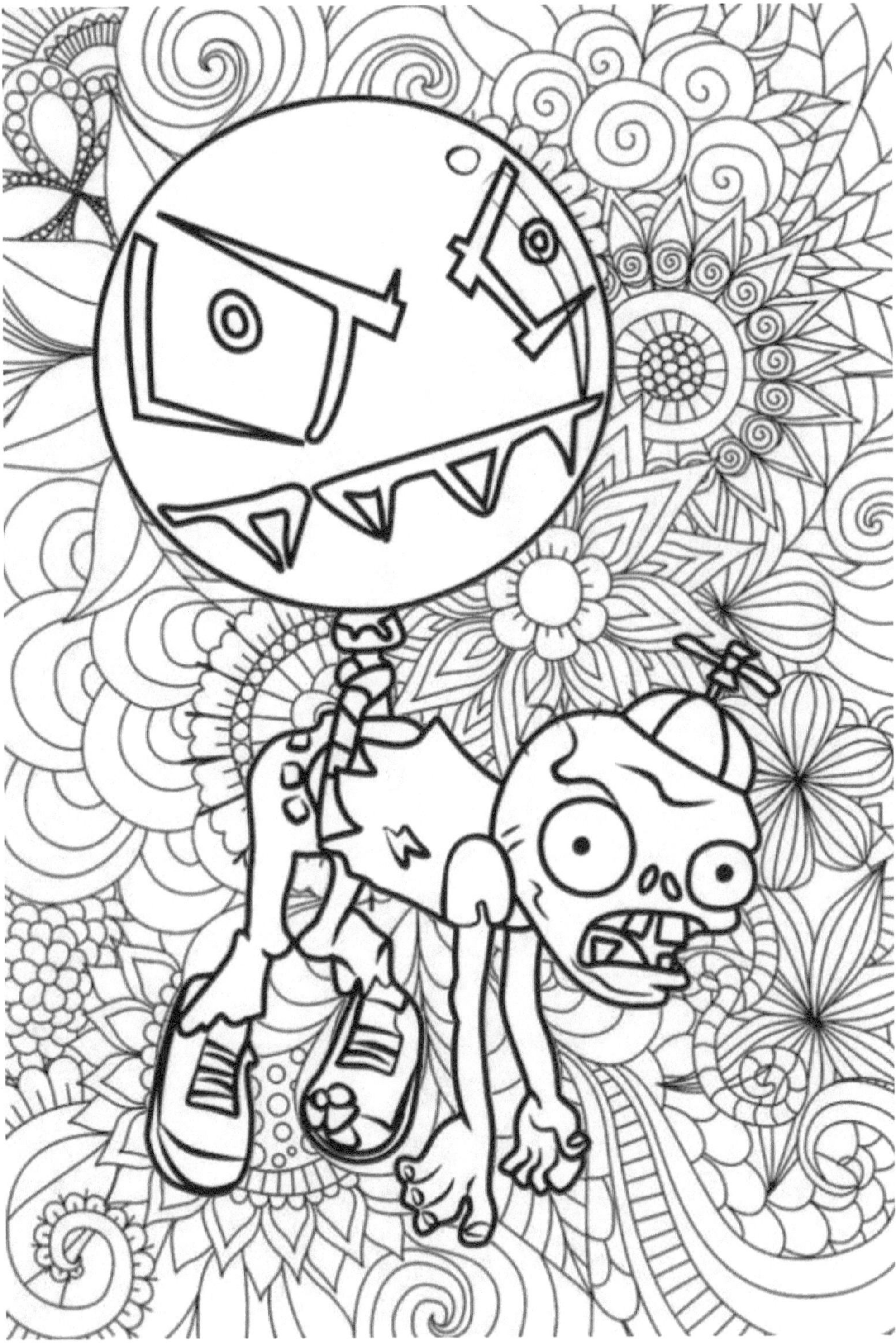

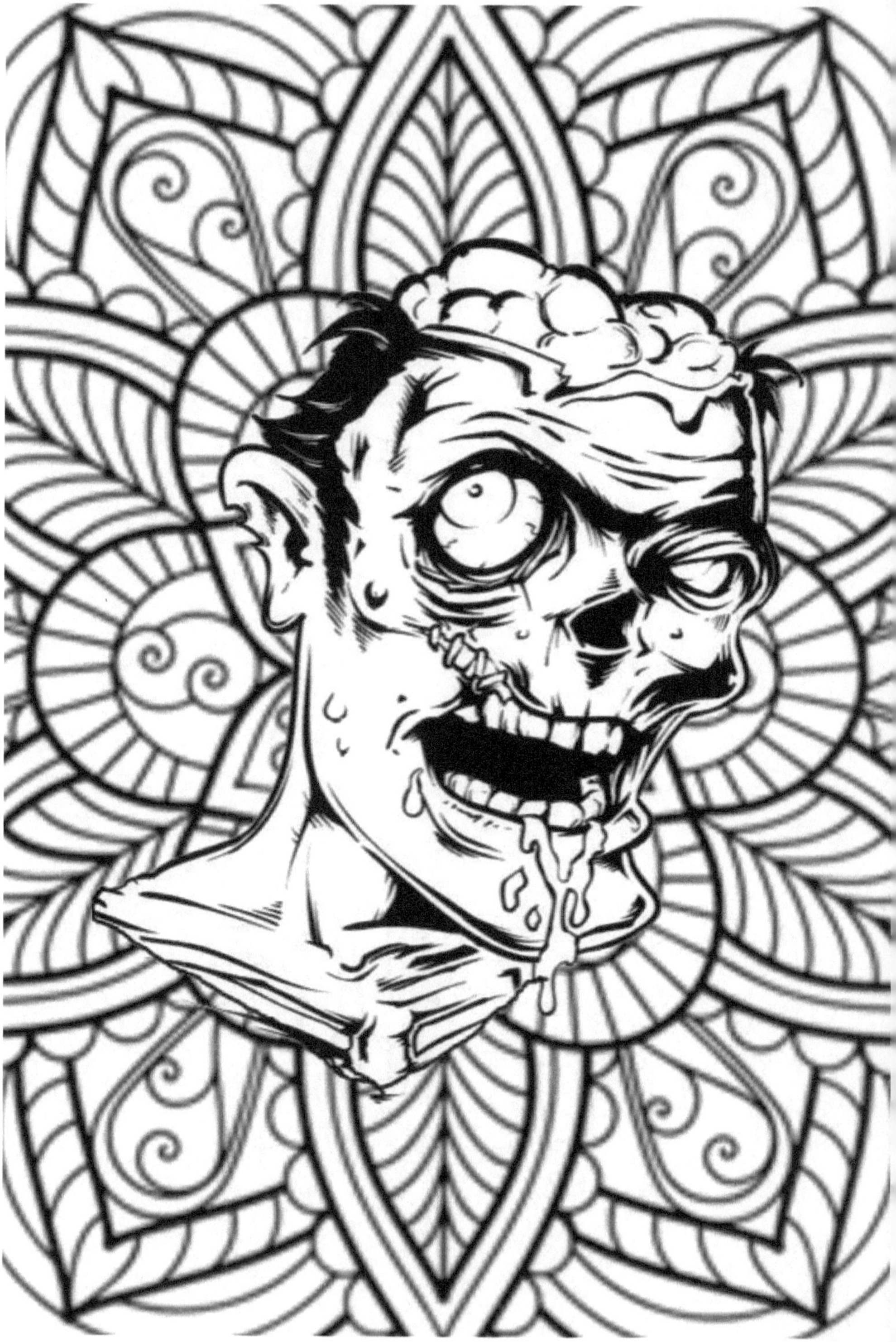

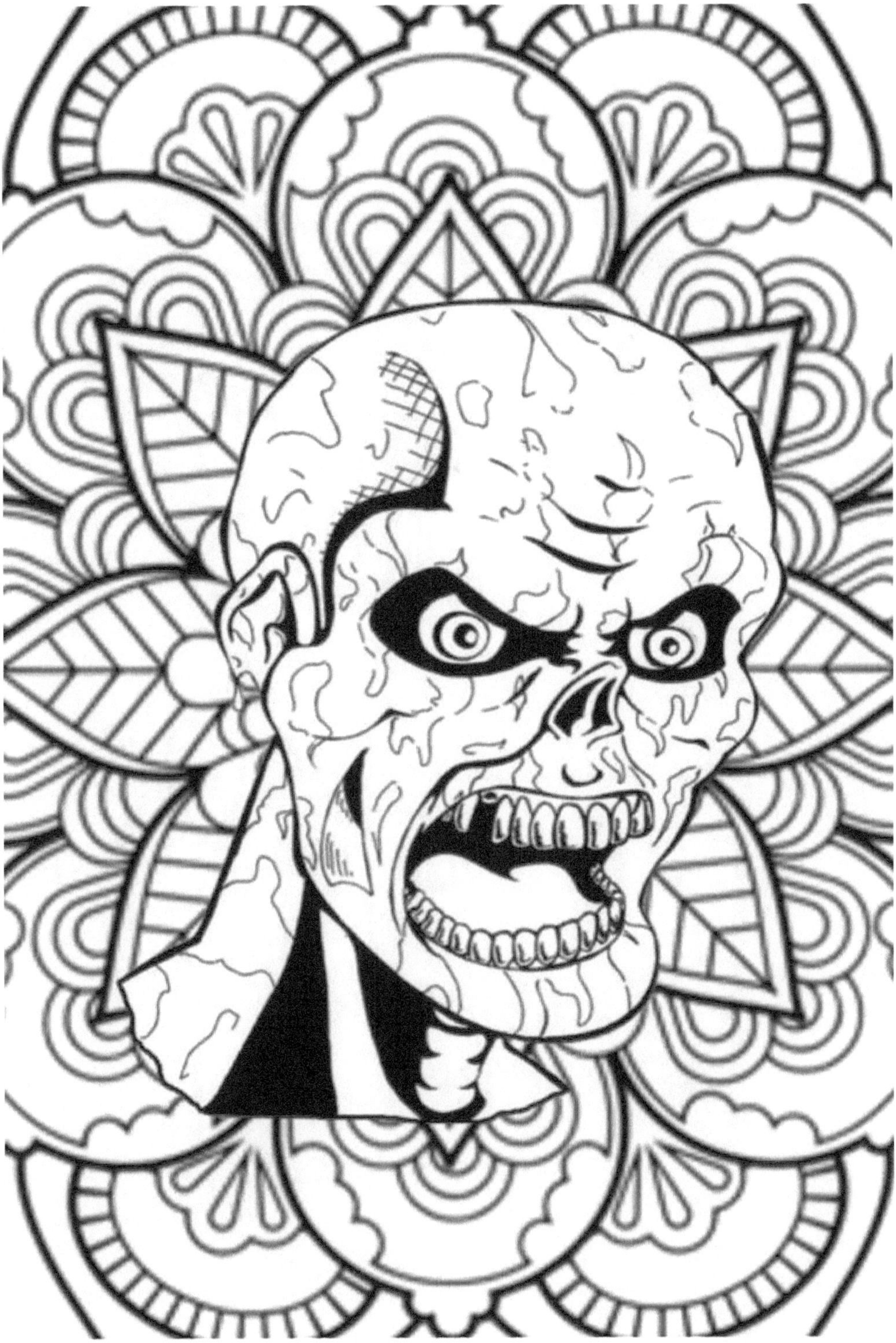

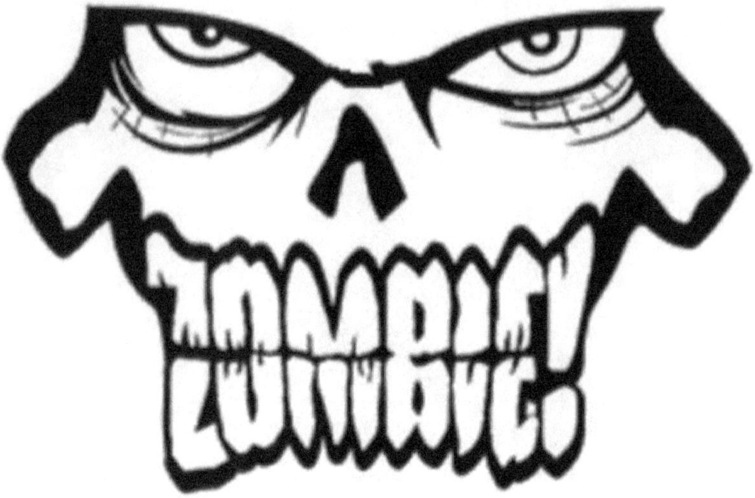
ZOMBIE!

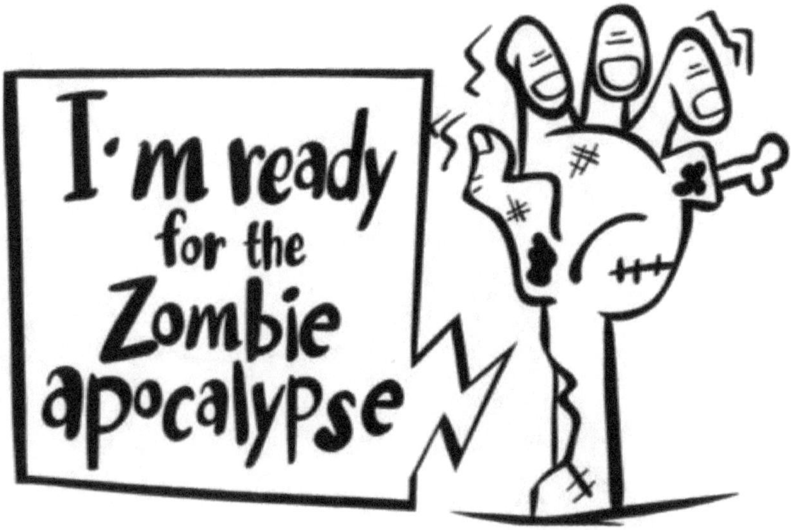
I'm ready for the Zombie apocalypse

www.ingramcontent.com/pod-product-compliance
Lightning Source LLC
Chambersburg PA
CBHW031509210526
45463CB00003B/1151
9781693837395